Francis Scott

Letters from a Layman to One who has left the Church of

England for that of Rome

Francis Scott

Letters from a Layman to One who has left the Church of England for that of Rome

ISBN/EAN: 9783744774789

Printed in Europe, USA, Canada, Australia, Japan

Cover: Foto ©Lupo / pixelio.de

More available books at **www.hansebooks.com**

LETTERS FROM A LAYMAN

TO

ONE WHO HAS LEFT THE CHURCH OF ENGLAND

FOR THAT OF ROME.

BY THE

HON. FRANCIS SCOTT.

𝔈𝔫𝔩𝔞𝔯𝔤𝔢𝔡 𝔈𝔡𝔦𝔱𝔦𝔬𝔫.

LONDON:

LONGMANS, GREEN, READER, AND DYER.

1869.

The following Letters, written in much sorrow, are published by request, and in the anxious hope that they may be of service in opening the eyes not only of him to whom they are addressed, but of others who, belonging to the Church of England and knowing little of that of Rome, are attracted by her forms and ceremonials, and fail to perceive the essential differences between the two.

LETTER I.

CANNES, ALPES MARITIMES,
March 1868.

MY DEAR FRANCIS,

I SOMEWHAT blame myself for not having spoken freely with you while here on the subject of your leaving the Church of England to adopt that of Rome. For whether you may heed my remarks or not, I have a duty to discharge. I have known and loved you all your life : I am your near relation and your Godfather, and therefore I ought not to remain silent. Moreover, we both believe in the same God ; we both trust in the same Mediator, Jesus Christ ; we both pray for grace from the same Comforter ; and we both hope for a joyful resurrection in the world to come. Whether you concede to me these privileges and blessings or not, I concede them all to you ; and I pray fervently that God may guide you and me aright.

As you were resolved to adopt the Romish Church, I rejoice that you go to Rome at once, for then and there you must ask yourself many serious questions, —Is this right ? is this true ? is this honest before God and man ? in regard to proceedings and observances which you will see and in which you may be called to take a part. Also, is there any warrant in Holy Writ for what you are doing, and what you see done by those who have taken vows to instruct in Religion and Christianity? I say Religion *and* Christianity, because you must ask yourself, Is this the Religion which Christ taught?

I have no doubt that you have both read and prayed much on the subject; and, as you say, "praying is better than thinking." True—but what has been your course of reading? what has been your intercourse with religious men? to what influences have you almost exclusively subjected yourself? have you "searched the Scriptures"[a] in order there to find the guidance of the Word of God; or have you not rather taken the ordinances of man? have you taken Holy Writ, and that alone, as the groundwork of the Church and the Church's teaching? Of late years have you not leant more to other teaching? have you of late years argued or consulted on the subject with any except those whose tendencies were towards extreme ceremonial and outward show? have you not avoided discussion with men who had not that bias?

The step you have taken, I infer from your remark, is the result of prayer. The man who takes his boat into the middle of the stream and prays instantly that it may not drift downwards, will remain as stationary as you were likely to do under similar circumstances in the Church of England.

Our daily prayer is not "Lead us into temptation and take care of us when there," but "Lead us not into temptation." I cannot wonder that, having volunteered to expose yourself to the attractions of a system which I consider a masterpiece of human mechanism, you should have yielded to the charm as others have done before you. But ask yourself again, Does Christ teach this? is there any warrant for this

[a] St John v. 39.

in either Gospels or Epistles ? or is not the warrant quite the other way ? Your doctrine is, that the Church of Rome is *the* Church, and you do not, because she does not, allow salvation out of her pale.

In Holy Writ we hear of the Church at Jerusalem, at Antioch where the disciples were first called Christians, at Corinth, and elsewhere, as well as at Rome.

Your doctrine and hers is, that the Church of Rome cannot err. Well, if St Peter could err himself, and be rebuked by our Lord " for savouring the things that be of men and not of God,"[b] even while the Lord was present with him, the successors of St Peter have had little chance to escape error. If St Peter could thrice deny his Lord on that dread night, there is much fear that those who pretend to inherit His faith may " crucify the Son of God afresh, and put Him to an open shame." [c] If even after the day of Pentecost St Peter could so err as to compel his brother apostle St Paul " to withstand him to the face because he was to be blamed,"[d] can you expect the Papacy to escape blame, or to possess that infallibility or security from error which did not belong to St Peter ?

On that beautiful address by our Lord to St Peter, " Thou art Peter, and on this rock will I build My Church ; and the gates of hell shall not prevail against it. And I will give unto thee the keys of the kingdom of heaven : and whatsoever thou shalt bind on earth shall be bound in heaven : and whatsoever thou shalt loose on earth shall be loosed in heaven ;"[e] on this, which has no reference to primacy, and on that other saying (like St Peter's denial, thrice repeated),

[b] St Matt. xvi. 23.   [c] Heb. vi. 6.

[d] Gal. ii. 11.   [e] St Matt. xvi. 18.

"Feed My sheep,"[f] does Rome rest her whole claim to supremacy. It is indifferent to me whether that "rock" meant St Peter, or the faith that "Thou art the Christ, the Son of the living God."[g] The Church of God is founded on a rock, and the gates of hell shall not prevail against it—and what has that to do with Rome, whither it is doubtful if St Peter ever went? It is a noble tribute to that great apostle to whom the remark is personally made, as was that other affecting prophecy addressed to him, "When thou shalt be old thou shalt stretch forth thy hands, and another shall gird thee, and carry thee whither thou wouldest not."[h] He too, the "apostle of the Circumcision," in his own person fulfilled the prophecy of unlocking "the kingdom of heaven"[i] by opening it to Cornelius and his household,[k] and by preaching the Gospel to the "lost sheep" of the house of Israel (*vide* note, p. 30): he was commissioned to bind and loose, but so were all the apostles.[l]

No construction of these passages, either singly or collectively, can give supremacy to Rome over other Churches.

If, however, Rome assume this address to St Peter as applicable to herself, she must also equally assume the address to St Peter five verses lower in the same sixteenth chapter of St Matthew: "Get thee behind Me, Satan; thou art an offence (or stumbling-block) unto Me; for thou savourest not the things that be of God, but those that be of men."[m]

Do you remember that Christ called the Twelve before Him in consequence of their dispute about superiority, and said to them, "If any man desire to

---

[f] St John xxi. 16.　　[g] St Matt. xvi. 16.　　[h] St John xxi. 18.
[i] St Matt. xvi. 19.　　[k] Acts x. 34.　　[l] St Matt. xviii. 18.
[m] St Matt. xvi. 23.

be first, the same shall be last of all, and servant of all ?" [n] And have you never turned to that beautiful description by St John at Patmos of the "twelve foundations of the wall, and in them the names of the twelve apostles of the Lamb ?" [o]

All this reference to other Churches you ignore. Confounding a part with the whole, you contend that the Church of Rome is the whole Church. All Scripture is against this perversion of truth. Have you also forgotten the Revelation of St John, where, in the last verse but five of the whole Bible, it is proclaimed, "I Jesus have sent Mine angel to testify unto you these things in the Churches ?" [p] You contend that the sound doctrines of Christianity can only be truly and safely taught in and by the Church of Rome; where do you find that laid down in Holy Writ? We perceive that the first and greatest apostles erred; and we learn that they differed or quarrelled; for we find "St Paul withstanding St Peter to the face;" "Barnabas carried away with dissimulation" (Gal. ii 11–13), and then the contention was so sharp between Paul and Barnabas that they parted, one going one way, the other the other, Paul taking with him Silas, and Barnabas taking Mark. It is, however, a significant fact that we are not informed who was right; and therefore it may appear that, in matters not set forth in Scripture, the right of private judgment rested with these fishers and tentmakers who inculcated Christ and Him crucified as the Captain of Salvation, and who taught that "there is none other name under Heaven given among men whereby we must be saved." [q]

[n] St Mark ix. 35.
[p] Rev. xxii. 16.
[o] Rev. xxi. 14
[q] Acts. iv. 12.

At Rome you will be able to judge whether there is any resemblance between the primitive proceedings and simple faith of the apostles, and the military parade and princely pomp of him who styles himself the Vicegerent of God upon earth. You will see the Holy Father, "servus servorum Dei," with the triple tiara on his head, signifying, as was assumed eight centuries ago, that he is crowned king of heaven, earth, and hell.

The teaching to which you subscribe being that the Roman Church cannot err, her pretensions where opposed to Scripture are right, and Scripture wrong. If it cannot err, and with it rest the infallible depositories of Divine truth, all that it has ever done or asserted, to that it must still adhere ; for in ceasing to maintain what it has once asserted, it convicts itself of error or of falsehood.

You lament, and so do I, the unseemly differences in the Church of England, and the lack of authority to control, or order to decide, what is right in matters of discipline and doctrine too. I believe that these discords in the Church you have left had much weight in inducing you to leave it, and to seek a refuge, as it were, where discipline was more strict ; and that finding this enforced at Rome, you have gone thither thinking there you discover uniformity. The uniformity you adhere to is the uniformity of infallibility. If, therefore, the Romish Church cannot maintain every iota or tittle of doctrine or assumption which it has ever in the course of ages asserted, you have united yourself to the uniformity of error. Be not shocked, the inference is logical, the sequence is necessary.

You will reply to me that in regard to questions of

doctrine and of discipline there are many matters of minor importance which are left open; and if one only belongs to the Church there is ample latitude afforded. We will consider these minor matters shortly.

Do you say it is not necessary to invoke saints, it is not an article of faith to address prayers to the Virgin?

I know the way they nurse you and lead you on;—milk to young babes. You are not yet fit to receive the whole faith. Thus you are drawn onward until you adopt and advocate the entire system of the present priestly power of granting indulgences for sin in the living, of pardoning men when they have sinned; of redeeming—literally re-d-emption or buying out souls after death by priests' prayers granted for money paid; of purgatory; of mediation by the merits of dead men, sinners like ourselves, in behalf of the dead with the " only Mediator between God and men, the Man Christ Jesus."ʳ The discipline which you have adopted as the cure for want of discipline here, compels you to adopt not only all this, but far more than all this in your search not for unity but for uniformity. There is just as much want of unity in doctrine among the Jesuits, Dominicans, and Franciscans as there is among members of the Church of England on points on which their differences are lamentable; but you have found uniformity at the awful sacrifice of abandoning Divine truths as laid down in the Old and New Testament for the doctrines adopted in later ages by the Church of Rome.

I have referred to the difference which arose be-

ʳ 1 Tim. ii. 5.

tween Paul and Barnabas when they separated;[s]
I have alluded to several churches named by the
apostles : but your doctrine being that the Pope's
is the only true Church, and that the Church of
Rome cannot err, let me ask you to refer to the
Epistles and tell me if the Church of the Galatians
could not also be a true Church?

Tell me too if St Peter must have been right in
giving way to those who insisted on the circumcision
of the Gentiles ; and, if so, why his followers do not
adopt the rite?

It would really appear as if warning were given
us against the very customs, practices, and doctrines
to which you are subscribing, by the following facts,
such as the enumeration, amongst others, of the
many churches, assigning to none the superiority—
in the declaration that "a man is justified by faith,
without the deeds of the law,"[t]—in the remark of
our Lord to His mother at the feast of the marriage
in Cana—in His observation that those who obey
His Word are His mother, and sister, and brother—
in the exclamation from the Cross addressed as much
to St John as to the Virgin—in the silence of
Scripture as to the Virgin afterwards, (the one
incidental notice of " the mother of Jesus with His
brethren " being present *after* mentioning each of the
apostles by name, " and the women " forming the sole
exception—in the contentions which existed between
St Peter, St Paul, and the other apostles—in the
declaration that he that would be greatest shall be
least—in the rebuke given to St Peter on one occasion—in the narrative of his fall and denial of his
Lord at the awful scene of the judgment hall—in

[s] Acts xv.   [t] Rom. iii. 20 ; Gal. ii. 16.

the desertion of their Master by the disciples at His crucifixion. All these events are recorded for our learning, and ought to humiliate us : and these records and other matters to which I shall allude presently, ought to make you pause, and pray, and think, and tremble.

Your reading, your hearing, your intercourse generally of late has been of a character to elevate what in a restricted sense is styled the Church.

Now this word "the Church" as you hear and read it, is so unlike the Church as written and read in Scripture, that it neither is nor appears to be the same thing.

When, therefore, you pray to be guided aright, you must pray direct to God through Him alone who is the only Mediator between God and man,[u] with your Bible before you ; and thus praying yourself, you must on no pretence deny the Bible to others. It will not do to pray that you may have grace to guide others into divine truth, and then under the teaching of a Church, to refuse the light of the gospel to those you affect and undertake to enlighten and to teach.

Can you expect that prayer will be blessed or duly answered by God if you leave the oracles of God, to be guided by the devices of man ?

Where is your warrant for those very institutions on which the Romish Church rests — monasteries, celibacy, and other things, perhaps originally meant for good, but unsupported by God's Word ? Peter, your "first Pope," had a wife, and our Lord visited her house ;[x] and the Epistle to Timothy expressly recognises the marriage of the clergy, both bishops and

[u] 1 Tim. ii. 5.   [x] St Matt. viii. 14.

deacons, and their taking due care of their children and families.[y]

Where the warrant for withholding the Bible, in defiance of the command, "Search the Scriptures; for they are they which testify of Me?"[z] Where that for denying the cup at the Holy Communion, in spite of the express injunction, "Drink ye *all* of this"?[a]

Where your warrant for prayer in an unknown tongue, in defiance of the gift of tongues by the Holy Spirit on the day of Pentecost, and against the whole fourteenth chapter of St Paul's First Epistle to the Corinthians? He tells you, in so doing, "your understanding is unfruitful, and cannot edify."[b] He in charity says you may "be judged mad" for so doing; but if you wilfully persist in doing it, may you not incur a severer sentence?

In obedience to the doctrines of the Church of Rome, you say, there is no salvation in the Church of England. Where, again, is your or their warrant for this condemnation? Is it of us that the apostle writes that "The Spirit speaketh expressly, that in the latter times some shall depart from the faith, giving heed to seducing spirits, and doctrines of devils; speaking lies in hypocrisy; . . . forbidding to marry, and commanding to abstain from meats, which God hath created to be received with thanksgiving of them which believe and know the truth?"[c]

Is it us especially that he bids to "refuse profane and old wives' fables, and exercise ourselves rather unto godliness?"[d]

Would it not be wise on this occasion, before the sweeping condemnation of the Church of England and

---

[y] I Tim. iii.   [z] St John v. 39.   [a] St Matt. xxvi. 27.
[b] I Cor. xiv.   [c] I Tim. iv. 1-3.   [d] *Ibid.* 7.

other Churches, for that of Rome to follow our Lord's advice, first to take the beam out of its own eye, that it may see clearly to take the mote out of its brother's eye ? [e]

You say many matters are minor, and therefore the Church does not regulate them. Now this is strange, that it can regulate the greater and not the less. One would have thought that an infallible Church would have completed the structure by regulating the whole.

Our Church lays claim to no infallibility; and therefore in its omissions, whether right or wrong, in disputed matters, it is less inexcusable than that which, assuming infallibility in all matters, asserts or omits to assert, as from time to time may suit its purposes.

Are things classed minor or otherwise according to the standard of God's law, or by human regulation ? What are these minor matters ? Are they such as mariolatry and hagiolatry ? Is the worship of the Virgin or of saints in obedience to God's law ? Minor are they ? How can things enjoined or forbidden in Holy Writ be minor or indifferent in the eye of any Church but one which disregards the injunctions or prohibitions it contains ?

If the first commandment teaches to worship God only,[f] the second is directed against idolatry. In that the New Testament can add nothing to the Old. That is enough. It was never imagined that any Christian Church could teach, preach, or practise idolatry. But fearful lest the worship, not of men but of angels, should creep in, the apostle St Paul warns lest any man should "beguile into the worshipping of angels;"[g] and St John, in the last chapter of the Revelation, strikingly forbids the same: "I John

---

[e] St Matt. vii. 3, 4 ; St Luke vi.   [f] Exod. xx.   [g] Col. ii. 18.

saw these things and heard them. And when I had heard and seen, I fell down to worship before the feet of the angel which showed me these things. Then saith he unto me, See thou do it not: for I am thy fellow-servant, and of thy brethren the prophets, and of them which keep the sayings of this book : worship God."[h]

Again, St Paul cautions the Colossians lest any man "spoil them through philosophy and vain deceit, after the tradition of men, after the rudiments of the world, and not after Christ."[i]

I conjure you to inquire whether, in this regard, the Church of Rome, which condemns us as unsound, does not teach for doctrines the commandments of men, and does not make the commandments of God of none effect through its traditions.[k]

You will find that the Church of your adoption teaches in its Catechism that " the authority of tradition is as great as that of Scripture, because," it says, "tradition came to us as well as Scripture from the apostles." Is this a fact ? What do you gain by tracing tradition to the apostles ? St John (xxi. 23) mentions a tradition respecting his own death, "a saying which went abroad among the brethren," regarding an expression of our Lord, to " testify " that reliance cannot be placed even upon apostolic tradition. While teaching this you will remember that in God's Word it is said, "Without is whosoever loveth or maketh a lie."[l]

I know it will be insinuated that it is not a positive doctrine with Rome to worship by adoration the men whom she has canonised,; that the saints only drop into their proper places in the order of devotion, and only take their due position in the matter of belief, so that their worship is the worship not of adoration but of honour.

This casuistry is subtle, but is not in accordance with your public teaching or public practice. The tree is known by its fruits.[m] Is it, then, worship or not worship? Are prayers addressed to the Virgin and to the saints, or are they not? I care not which. If worship, how reconcile it with the Bible? If not worship, how reconcile it with what, after taking the Bible from them, you lead or mislead your people to believe?

Your prayers, your professions, your proclamations, your processions all tend to and produce the belief in the efficacy of the mediation of saints, to the displacing of our Lord from His one mediatorial throne, to the sharing of His power by departed sinners invoked by others living, to the eclipsing of Christ's glory, and the doubt of the mercy and justice, the faithfulness and love of the declared only advocate[n] with God the Father, who said, " Come unto ME, all ye that labour and are heavy laden, and I will give you rest." [o]

Henceforth you are to learn and to teach to address the Virgin as the Queen of heaven, and, as all-powerful with Jesus Christ, to ask her to give you her patronage and protection with Him. What is this but a blasphemous mistrust of the three great attributes of the Godhead, infinite power, infinite wisdom, and infinite mercy?

You are also by the process of development in the system of tradition to believe in and to teach that

[m] St Matt. vii. 20.   [n] 1 John ii. 1.   [o] St Matt. xi. 28.

which the infallible Church invented a few years ago, the immaculate conception of the Blessed Virgin; and you are to pretend that God revealed this fact in Holy Writ, though no one, not even your Church, knows when or how it was revealed, or how it was found out only about ten years ago. This is an article of your new faith, against which your Church at Candlemas annually adduces a standing witness in the "Feast of the Purification." Wherefore, should Mary, if free from original sin, offer the ordained sin-offering?[p] Why, with nothing to atone for, make an atonement?[q] Thus your Church disproves her own doctrine.

But why do you stop with the Blessed Virgin? Do you leave it for a further discovery to find out that the parents of the Virgin Mary enjoyed the same immunity? There is equal scriptural warrant for believing this of them, and quite as much reason for the belief that the exception mounted up through successive generations until it reached the inspired Psalmist. The Saviour was proclaimed Son of David. Your Church (as well as ours, which you style no Church) addresses our Lord by that title. He Himself claims this address as belonging to Him; there is therefore on many grounds reason to assign this dignity to king David if assignable to the Virgin; but you see to what absurdities these impostures lead.

As the preceding doctrine detracts from the Saviour's Godhead, so this disparages the Redeemer's manhood. The former leaves a doubt on the mind of him who prays, whether the intercessory prayer may ever reach the Throne of Grace, or reach it in due

[p] Lev. xii. 8.   [q] St Luke ii.

time. The latter takes from the mourner or the tempted half his joy ; his comfort or peace in believing. Thus both are not only unholy, but cruel doctrines.

In the first case, the saint, as Elijah said, " may be talking, or he may be pursuing, or is on a journey, or peradventure he sleepeth, and must be awaked," [r] or he may be pleading for another, and you must wait.

In the second case, the Messiah being born of a woman who was free from the condemnation of our first parents, He could not derive from her or take upon Him the weakness of our nature, and therefore could not be subject to our frailties. We have *not* [in Christ] an high priest which can be touched with the feeling of our infirmities, or in all things tempted like as we are; [s] we can *not* therefore come boldly unto the Throne of Grace, that we may obtain mercy, and find grace to help in time of need, as we had hoped to obtain from the " man Christ Jesus." [t]

Thus Incarnation defeats its own purpose.

What an awful doctrine is this !

But beyond all this, you proclaim miracles wrought not only by men canonised by Rome, but by their effigies, in wood, in stone, in metal, or on canvas. What is more common than for a particular church to have a momentary reputation for some miracle reputed to have been recently wrought there ? I remember one effigy of the Virgin bringing much profit to a particular church at Rome while I was there, and another blessed saint serving his shrine in like manner. Go and inquire for winking pictures of the Virgin. Go and see the waxen figure of the " blessed

[r] 1 Kings xviii. 27.   [s] Heb. iv. 15, 16.   [t] 1 Tim. ii. 5.

B

Lorenzo" at Rome, reported miraculously to be real undecaying and undecayed flesh. Go also to Naples and see the annual miraculous liquefaction of the blood of St Januarius ; and tell me if it be a pure religion which thus practises a gross idolatry and deceit, believed by the people whom you therefore keep in ignorance. May we not say, "They have not known nor understood : for he hath shut their eyes, that they cannot see ; and their hearts, that they cannot understand. And none considereth in his heart, neither is there knowledge nor understanding to say, I have burned part of it in the fire ; yea, also I have baked bread upon the coals thereof ; I have roasted flesh, and eaten it : and shall I make the residue thereof an abomination ? shall I fall down to the stock of a tree ? He feedeth on ashes : a deceived heart hath turned him aside, that he cannot deliver his soul, nor say, Is there not a lie in my right hand ?"[u]

It is in vain to tell me these idols are not objects of veneration and of worship to the Roman and Romish people—see them "bow down to them, and worship them."[x] Go to St Peter's and observe the "molten image" near the high altar, formerly, they say, a statue of Jupiter, an object of heathen adoration at Rome; but now of St Peter, an equal object of worship among the benighted people. Watch them kiss and rub the foot with their mouths, their hands, and faces, as if they perceived that virtue went out of it ;[y] until the metal of this molten image is in part actually worn away by constant devotion. If this be not idolatry, it is far removed from a pure and holy worship, and can never be pleasing in the eyes of a "jealous God."[z]

" It must needs be that offences come, but woe to that man by whom the offence cometh." [a]

Are not these impostures destroying souls, more fatal than heathen sacrifices which destroyed bodies? What, let me ask, do you intend by the sacrifice of the Mass? is it a sacrifice? was the one oblation " once made when Christ offered up Himself for the sins of the whole world," [b] an insufficient sacrifice?

" Behold, to obey is better than sacrifice ; and to hearken than the fat of rams." [c]

Are you blind guides leading the blind ; or, with open eyes, do you blind and deceive others?

If the first, take then the beam from your eyes.

If the second, remember the words, " Scribes and Pharisees, hypocrites! ye compass sea and land to make one proselyte, and when he is made, ye make him twofold more the child of hell than yourselves : . . . . ye outwardly appear righteous unto men, but within ye are full of hypocrisy and iniquity." [d]

Again, what is the teaching of indulgences? Is that, too, minor? Is that also in accordance with Divine law? The Church of Rome cannot err ; and therefore, as you learn and as you teach, all it has done is right, and may and should be done again. " Semper eadem." The end justifies the means. Indulgences sold for money are and have been an awful but useful source of profit to the Church. The stately basilica of St Peter at Rome was built in part from sums obtained by the sale of indulgences. In this manner and for this purpose indulgences were sold to those who kept and those who resorted to taverns, wine-shops, dancing-rooms, and places of worse repute. Was this no error? Were they not licenses to the devil for the glory and honour of God? Yet this was sanctioned and used by the true and infallible Church.

These, forsooth, are minor matters! and you profess obedience. Minor! Eating an apple was minor! nay, it was represented as not only of no importance, but positively good, pleasant, desirable, making wise. But it was disobedience to God, and was the cause of all our woe.

See that what you follow or omit as "minor" and as "desirable to make you wise"[e] be not equally a disobedience to the oracles of God, which alone have the doctrines of salvation.

I have heard it said, "How strange that clergymen should so often go over to Rome!" I have always replied, I see nothing more strange in them, but rather less strange than in other men going over, not because they read the Scriptures more or less, but because they read the writings of uninspired ecclesiastical authors recounting the lives of men canonised during the dark ages, and admire the history of the Church invested with vast temporal as well as spiritual power.

There is nothing so dazzling as ambition, so attractive as the possession of authority, or so natural to young minds as the love of power. No power is so great as that over the soul; none so easily attainable as that dominion which ordination into priests' orders in your Church is asserted to give over the souls of men dead or alive.

Such is the teaching, not of the Word of God, but of the Church of Rome, which therein is directly antagonistic to God's Word.

[e] Gen. iii. 6.

Nothing is so subtle as the argument used ; nothing so fascinating as the result reached ; and I assure you that if in my conscience I could only in part bring myself to believe that there was any truth or soundness in these doctrines, there is something so comforting, so consoling, so delightfully enjoyable in the idea, that I should at once become a Romish priest, or at least a Romanist. I should hope, if rich enough, to enjoy a life of pleasure here and compound for it with the priest hereafter.

It would be preferable to be a priest, because I should not only take care of myself, but be paid for taking care of others.

If that assertion appear broad, I could at any rate obtain from the men ordained to officiate for the purpose, that relief here and redemption hereafter which the Church that cannot err alone awards. Is the Psalmist then in *error*, when he says that this cannot be done by money or by man ? Have you forgotten the 49th Psalm, " There be some that put their trust in their goods, and boast themselves in the multitude of their riches : but no man may deliver his brother, nor make agreement unto God for him : for it cost more to redeem their souls, so that he must let that alone for ever."[f]

No wonder that the Church of Rome, claiming freedom from error, selling indulgences and granting absolution, should keep back from the people the Word of God which thus condemns the word of man.

I said I was glad you had gone to see Rome, and I particularly urge you not to miss seeing all the imposing ceremonies of Easter.

You will remember that St John says that our

[f] Ps. xlix. 6-8.

Saviour at the Passover, after supper, "laid aside His garments, and took a towel and girded Himself, and washed His disciples' feet, and wiped them with the towel wherewith He was girded."[g] This remains to us an example of the humility of the Man-God, our Master and Lord.

I beg you to go and see the representation of this in the present day. The effect is dramatic if not reverential; and you will judge in what guise this mark of our Lord's humility is perpetuated every Easter in Rome to beggars who come into a church at night for the purpose; and then ask yourself if it be not a mockery rather than a mark of respect, and an example of the pride which apes humility.

You have asserted the Church of England to be, according to the teaching of Rome, no Church, and therefore having no salvation. But our doctrines are without exception the early doctrines of the primitive Christian Church as professed and practised at Rome and elsewhere in purer days. Generally our morning and evening service, our collects and prayers, are those used in the Church of Rome;—and in accepting the negative term Protestant, we indicate our protest against tenets, or formularies, introduced in later ages, and which Scripture neither warrants nor supports. Christianity being founded on the Word of God, Christian Churches other than that of Rome adhere to the command, "Search the Scriptures;—they are they which testify of Me." Rome forbids this search; but other Churches, finding therein the mandate "Him only shalt thou serve,"[h] as to the worship of God and the prohibition to worship others, object to the teaching of a Church which, in defiance of God's Word, can

[g] St John xiii. 4, 5.   [h] St Matt. iv. 10.

lengthen the Creed or shorten the Commandments. The Church of Rome does both, and boasts of the power to do so, under the unfounded doctrine of infallibility;—a doctrine, like many others of purely human invention, supported by the plausible argument of development. That which nineteen centuries ago was good enough for the ignorant fishermen on the shores of the Sea of Tiberias, or the illiterate converts of Greece or Rome, is totally unsuited to the advanced period of education in which we live. Men forget what the Messiah quoted to the Scribes and Pharisees of that day, " Out of the mouth of babes and sucklings Thou hast perfected praise." [1]

The Church of Rome, and you as a conscientious and dutiful member of the same, boast that you are followers of St Peter. It would be a nobler aim to boast that members of His Church were followers of Christ.

The apostle St Paul appears to have anticipated and foreshadowed such a following of others rather than of Christ, when he remarks, " You say, I am of Paul, I am of Apollos, I am of Cephas, and I of Christ ; " and then asks, "Is Christ divided ?" [k] showing that the Church should be a Christian Church, as under Christ and not as under man.

I know that you declare that "devotion to God claims an obedience above devotion to anything else," and you act on the declaration. It is an admirable sentiment, and, rightly directed, a noble duty. For this obedience you have left kindred, have deserted friends, have avoided acquaintance, and given up society ; for this you have shunned advice from others, and concealed from them your own opinions ; you

[1] St Matt. xxi. 16.   [k] 1 Cor. i. 12.

have subjected yourself to strict rules and observances ; you have yielded up to your superiors your
right of private judgment, and allowed your private
correspondence to be opened and read by them.

You have done more than this. For this sentiment,
you, a priest of the Church of England, of mature age,
baptized into Christ in that faith, and having baptized
others, have abjured it,—have admitted that neither
you nor I nor those before you were Christians,—have
been baptized afresh, having fresh sponsors at this
your new baptism.

How noble, if right : how sad and terrible, if in all
things you, fancying you are obeying God, are only
subjecting yourself to the ordinances of men ! You
have done all this for the doctrine of obedience.
Obedience to whom or to what ? To God—to God's
Word ? No ! Obedience to man ! obedience to the
Bishop of Rome, God's Vicegerent on earth, as he
blasphemously says ; devotion and obedience to a man,
the self-styled representative of God, of whose doctrines we may say, that when the Word of God is at
variance with the Church of Rome, it is not the
Church of Rome but the Word of God that must give
way. You hold all teaching but that of Rome to be
false ; all her teaching to be true.

You, as a Romanist, hold that man's truest and
divine life flows alone through yourselves ; as sap
through the tree or blood supplying the human body.
This we do not deny you, though you deny it us.
You proceed to say that I am spiritually dead,
withered as a branch cut from the tree, lopped from
the true Vine,[1] hopeless, helpless, and lost to salvation ; not because I fail to believe in Christ through

---

[1] St John xv. 6.

the apostle's word, or to hold the doctrines of the Bible and perform the duties of Christianity, or because not baptized into Christ in the name of the Trinity;—but because I am not joined to the Church of Rome. I ask, is that charity, or is there any scriptural authority for such condemnation? No! but it is the true doctrine and consistent conduct of that Church which cannot err.

In proof of this, go to the Pope's mint at the Vatican, and buy a copy of the medal struck and preserved in commemoration of the event so worthy to be remembered in Romish history—the massacre of St Bartholomew, when many thousand Protestants were murdered ; having an appropriate obverse and legend, " Strages Ugonottorum," Slaughter of the Huguenots. I got the medal there, and I have it still.

Go also to the vestibule of that most sacred part of the palace of God's Vicegerent, the Sistine Chapel, and behold in the life-like, life-sized fresco, this treacherous massacre, with the murdered Coligni depicted. The inscription which was beneath it, and described it, has of late years been erased on account of the scandal it afforded to many who visited the place. (*Vide* note, p. 30).

You may hear, you may believe, and say that in these respects, if the doctrines of the Church of Rome be not changed, her practice is modified, that she no longer denies the Bible, nor persecutes those who read it, or who differ from her.

I remember on one night an armed band of soldiers, sent at the instigation of the bishop of the diocese, passing my house, to a quiet, peaceable village, situated in a remote mountainous district about ten miles off. They arrived there at midnight, and directed by the priest's servant, the soldiers surrounded the several houses ; they broke in, took the peasants from their beds, bound them savagely with thongs and cords, and tearing them from their families hurried them off by night, and casting them into a dark filthy prison, put with common malefactors these men, whose only alleged crime or cause for persecution was the possession of and hearing and reading the Holy Scriptures. I heard the charge, I saw their homes outraged and plundered by the soldiery, I learnt the sad tale from the anxious and terror-stricken women in the desolate village, and I visited the men in gaol.

This happened under the authority of the Romish Church in the nineteenth century, in one of the most devoted, if not devout, countries in her dominions. So do not tell me that when she has the power, and thinks she can do so with impunity, the Church of Rome is not the same everywhere as she has for ages been.

"Ex uno disce omnes :"—but if you are told this is exceptional, take another very simple test which is normal and universal, and in which you can be deceived neither as to the practice or effect of excluding and ignoring the Bible in countries belonging to the Latin Church. You know in England and most Protestant countries there is scarcely a bookseller's shop, however humble, in town or village where you may not buy a Bible or Testament.

Try to procure one in Romish countries. Go as I have done in Italy, France, and other places, ask of the principal booksellers in capitals and large towns, and you will ask in vain, and perhaps be met with the reply "Je ne tiens pas ces articles là !" articles of which there is neither supply nor demand! You may find the biography of some unknown saint, but a Testament or a portable Bible never. By what doctrine of development do you explain this inferiority of the Word of God?

Explain also to yourself, to me it would be more difficult, the meaning and value of the announcement, "Altare privilegiatum quotidianum," which you see written up constantly. Has a particular altar greater virtue than another? In what respect? and whence derived?

The Bible and a true Church inculcate what is right and true. A public inscription at Rome will tell you that, by authority of a certain Pope, whoever devoutly kisses a certain wayside cross "will obtain release from purgatory for many hundred (I think three hundred) years." Likewise, in another quarter, you learn that you may receive a like release from purgatory for, I think, some thousand years, through the merits of a dead man canonized by Rome.

This is cheap, and worth doing, if right; if wrong, it is a shameless imposture: but whether right or wrong, it is the doing of the Church of Rome at Rome, and I am glad you go there to see the system in full perfection.

Do not tell me I must look elsewhere than to the inscriptions in churches for the formularies of the Church,—that they may vary as is expedient. This, and far more than this, is its public practice, this its outward teaching. These are the practical doctrines which are intended to affect, and do affect the people and impose upon the laity, as the substitute for that Word of God which the Church forbids them to read. May I not then say that your "obedience" to such a system is not obedience to God, but obedience to man against God ?

Want of charity condemns as heretics the members of another Church ; want of truth releases from pains after death, on payment of a fee or kissing of a cross, a member of your own. Can you believe this ?

I have some misgivings whether you may be permitted to read this letter ; but I entreat you to give it such attention as you think a letter written from such a quarter on such a subject in true love and affection may deserve, and ask yourself how it is that, believing in the Author and Finisher of our faith, and trusting to Him as bearing the burden of our transgressions, I, striving with fear and trembling, have mistaken the grounds of my salvation.[m]

It is quite possible that you are somewhat influenced in your appreciation of the propriety of your joining the Church of Rome by the amount of sacrifice you made in so doing.

It is even probable that you may measure the duty by the sincerity of your present conviction.

I do not doubt that you have acted conscientiously ; but I should fail in my duty if I did not bid you beware how you trust to the soundness of these impressions. You will find many who will flatter and encourage you, who will praise you for what you have done, who will extol you for the sacrifice you have made.

This letter will find you surrounded with such adulation as will almost elevate you to martyrdom, or at least to the merit of one whose " good works " have made him suffer in the cause, I cannot say of Christ, but in the cause of the Church of Rome.

[m] Phil. ii. 12.

Beware of reliance on that which is called "good works," the satisfaction at which may be akin to spiritual pride. The definition, too, of that word "the Church" is dangerously elastic; often meaning the supremacy of temporal and spiritual power; sometimes the clergy without the laity; sometimes "docens;" sometimes "discens;" sometimes the sacred building; as may suit the casuist :—but rarely at Rome the congregation of faithful Christians. A subtle flexibility this in the mouths of Jesuits !

My letter will find you in the midst of learned and able divines, used to the casuistry of Bellarmine, versed in the doctrines of Romanism. I pretend to no knowledge on the subject beyond that which is open to all the laity in other Churches,—which is shut by the priesthood to the laity in yours.

I have been taught, and am still content to believe, that whether "Paul has planted, or Apollos watered, it is God that giveth the increase."[a] This you have been taught, and have taught the same to others. You are now forbidden to teach or preach this simple primitive faith, this apostolic doctrine ; but I fervently pray that God in His great mercy may open your eyes, may hold you to the faith, which I am satisfied you still believe though prohibited to preach, and may give you boldness, even now returning to God's Gospel, to make a sacrifice for Christ greater, nobler, and worthier far than that which you have made for the Church of Rome.

I am,

Yours with the sincerest affection,

FRANCIS SCOTT.

[a] 1 Cor. iii. 6.

NOTE to p. 6.

There is no certain evidence that St Peter, the Apostle " of the Circumcision," ever visited Rome. His last date is from Babylon, and all his allusions and references indicate that he addressed persons acquainted with Jewish history and Hebrew customs.

NOTE to p. 25.

Bunsen's work on Rome, vol. ii., on the Vatican, thus describes it:— " The painting to the right of the entrance of the Sistine Chapel refers, *as well as the two on the wall opposite the Pauline Chapel,* to the massacre of St Bartholomew. On the first, one sees the corpse of the murdered Coligny, but who has here the appearance of a living person dragged through the streets of Paris. The second represents the general massacre of the Protestants in that city, and on the right appears Charles IX. in Parliament for the purpose of justifying this, and confirming the condemnation of Coligny." The following were the inscriptions—1. " Massacre of the Huguenots ; " 2. " The King approves the Death of Coligny ; " 3. " Gaspar Admiral Coligny is carried home wounded. Gregory XIII. Sovereign Pontiff, MDLXXII."

LETTER II.

SENDHURST GRANGE, GUILDFORD,
June 1868.

My dear Francis,

A S regards myself, I cannot fail to be pleased alike
with the earnest tone and affectionate temper of
your reply to the letter I wrote on your adoption of
the Church of Rome. We both feel that neither the
subject nor the mode of treating it should be taken up
or set down lightly. I am therefore disposed to offer
some remarks on your observations. In doing this, I
cannot conceal from you the pain which your letter
has given me. It conveys to my mind the impression
that you have written under the advice, and perhaps
the dictation, of the priests who have for a time
gained an influence over your mind, and who have
succeeded in blinding your eyes to such an extent,
that you cannot see the fallacies which to any unpre-
judiced mind are transparent in your letter.

This is one of the unhappy marks of the lamentable
apostasy of later times ; the delusion is so strong
that a lie is believed.. Had you been as one of those
silly women or effeminate men who, ignorant of Holy
Scriptures and carried away by pompous ceremonial,
have lately joined the Church of Rome, as many of
the like station in society did in the time of Charles
the First, I should not have been surprised ; but that
one brought up in the knowledge of God's Holy Word,

ordained to the ministry of the reformed Church of England, pledged by solemn oath to its doctrines and principles, should have rushed precipitately into the superstition of idolatry and the Papacy, is to me, and to all who know you, a subject of amazement and of unutterable grief.

I cannot undertake to follow you through the detected platitudes and exploded commonplaces of the controversy, of which you have adduced so many, every one of which has again and again triumphantly been answered by converts from Popery at the time of the Reformation, and by converts of later and quite modern date. Some, however, I cannot pass over in silence, and especially two subjects upon which you lay great stress. The first, the Infallibility, the second, the Idolatry, of the Church of Rome. Can you in your conscience really believe the pretensions which the Church of Rome makes for the first, or can you possibly defend her practice as regards the second?

For example, as to infallibility. I have in vain searched through your arguments for proof that the Church of Rome is infallible. I desire to find the practical and tangible point where it is supposed to exist. Is it in the Pope?—if so, how comes it to pass that Popes have been declared to be fallible by other Popes, by most learned theologians, and by Councils? Is it in Councils?—how is it then, by the common consent of history that Councils have erred in matters of faith? Is it in the Church?—then you must define what you mean by the Church, which, if it be composed of clergy and laity, is not likely to have ever given, or ever to be in a position to give, a united, undivided, and infallible opinion upon any subject. You say, the Church gives authority to the Scriptures. Be it so for argument's sake. But the Church of Rome has not given more authority to the Scriptures than the Church of the Jews to the Old Testament, and yet no one would say that the Jews were infallible interpreters of Scripture. Critics may pronounce upon the authenticity of Thucydides or Aristotle, but differ widely in their interpretation of them. Rome may possess the Scriptures, and yet make them of none effect by the traditions of men.

You and Rome say, " If the Church of Rome be fallible, the New Testament is fallible ; if the Church be infallible, the New Testament is infallible," and you infer the converse. You say, " It is and must be so, because the Church of Rome testifies to Holy Writ."

The authenticity of Scripture rests on accumulated original, external, and internal evidence, from genuine sources of greatest antiquity more than all the works of Greek classical literature together can command. You mean that those who testify to the truth of the Bible, must be true and correct in all else that they assert.

The Jesuitry is ingenious, but the sophistry is transparent. By your rule, if you bear conclusive evidence to my title to an estate, you prove your own claim to another. By this rule, if you establish my hair to be one colour, you prove your own to be the same. " Who drives fat oxen must himself be fat." The truth is, that when this absurd claim to infallibility is analysed the Papist has not advanced one single step nearer to the idea of infallibility than the Protestant ; on the contrary, he has left the fountain of living waters for broken cisterns which will hold no water, and is exposed to the peril of trusting to an arm of flesh rather than to the Spirit of God. Let it be

c

tested by our experience in times of bitter conviction of sin, in humiliation under the heavy hand of chastening, in the prospect of death and judgment, whether on our bended knees and in our broken hearts we find any comfort from the decisions and decretals of a worldly-minded Pope, such as Hildebrand or Leo X., or in the verbal absolution of some poor sinful priest who perhaps himself has never experienced the powers of the new birth and found peace with God through Jesus Christ our Lord. Surely at such a moment the witness of the Holy Ghost, and the unchangeable Word of God is the only infallible source of comfort.

The infallibility of Rome is like the hypothesis of perpetual motion : no one has yet made the discovery where it is. The Church of Rome claims to be infallible, and asserts that the Holy Scriptures belong to her, that she has the sole charge of them, and the exclusive right to interpret them. Let us see how she has discharged her duty, executed her trust, and treated God's Word.

The Council of Trent, professing to act under Divine inspiration, and certainly acting with the sanction of the infallible Pope, declared the Vulgate Latin Translation authentic ("pro authenticâ habeatur"—Conc. Trid. 4 Sess.), and on no pretence to be rejected by any one. An edition was published in 1590, under Pope Sixtus V., and this edition is infallible and to be received as an article of faith.

In 1593, or three years afterwards, another infallible Pope, Clement VIII., published another authentic edition differing from the preceding.

How do you reconcile these contradictions ? I will not stop to ask you to compare any passages, *e.g.*, 1 Cor. iv. 6 in the Greek and Vulgate, nor will I refer to

St Augustine, who forbade St Jerome's Vulgate to be read in his churches, because it differed from the Septuagint.

Martini, a good Catholic authority, Archbishop of Florence, translated the New Testament in the last century, and states in his original edition, and in that of 1782-92, that in the authentic Vulgate 975 passages vary from the original Greek. The same admission of 975 errors in the Vulgate translation of the New Testament is repeated in the edition of 1854, printed with the approbation of Minucci, Archbishop of Florence. These are your own admissions, nor are these errors accidental. Cardinal Bellarmine thus answered a theologian (Luke of Bruges), who wrote to advise him of errors in the Vulgate which had escaped his notice and should be corrected : " I beg you to know that we have not most accurately corrected the Vulgate Bible, for we have carefully (or purposely), for good reasons (de industria justis de causis), passed over many passages which seemed to require correction." What excuse can be made for such allowance of error by such high authority ? Now follows the admission of the Chief Bishop, who would not err or mislead, and could not, if he would. It occurs in the Preface of the Vatican edition of the authentic Vulgate Bible of Pope Clement VIII. : " As some passages have been altered on purpose, so some which seemed to require alteration have on purpose been left unchanged" —" Sicut nonnulla consulto mutata, in etiam alia quae mutanda videbantur, consulto immutata relicta sunt." (*Vide* note, p. 75.)

The Romish Church claims to have the right to use the Scriptures which belong to her, and altering Holy

Writ under the holy authority of the Divine Spirit, she proceeds to disparage its value.

You assign reasons which affect to show that there would be no great harm if Rome did deny the Bible to her people, and that there is little or no need to read. Yet you betray an uncomfortable doubt as to whether, if she had so acted, Rome would not have made at least one mistake, and you proceed accordingly to assert that it is not true. In proof of your assertion, you assure me that you, a Protestant priest, who went over to Rome with the Bible in your hand, are permitted to keep it, and that it is daily read among you ; as if its possession by you, a convert from the Church of England, or its reading in your cloisters, were any proof that it is not buried there, and generally withheld from members of the Church of Rome. In what language do you read it ?

You say the Bible is not prohibited. But Popes and Councils are infallible, and, so long ago as 1229, we have the decree of the Council of Toulouse, under Gregory IX.: " We prohibit to the laity the books of the Old and New Testament, unless some one for devotion desires perhaps a Psalter or Breviary for divine offices, and the Hours of the Blessed Virgin ; but these they may not have translated." (*Vide* note, p. 75.)

You may say that is a long while ago. Is it changed ? Rome never changes ; and, alas ! she cannot change until she surrenders her unfounded claim to infallibility.

It is possible that you may cavil with the Council of Toulouse as being a *Provincial* Council and therefore not infallible. As to infallibility, I will give you the benefit of the doubt. But that does not raise any question either on the commencement or the continuance of the practice of proscribing the Bible, for reading which Rome burnt persons alive in Spain, in France, in Germany, in England, in the Low Countries, and elsewhere.

The Church of Rome, in the heading to the fourth Rule of the Index Expurgatorius, states that "from the reading of the Bible comes more harm than good."

I refer you to pages 30, 94, 177, 258, 269, 272, and 273 of the Index under the pretended authority of the Holy Ghost, to see whether Rome permits or prohibits the Bible.

The celebrated Papal Bull Unigenitus, of Clement XI., in 1713, which is in force in these dominions, certainly in Ireland, declares, among other things, that reading the Bible is neither useful nor necessary, and that laymen ought not to read the Bible on Sundays, or that to take the Gospel from the hands of the people, or give it them closed, i.e., in unknown tongue, is not shutting the mouth of Jesus Christ. (80–4.)

Where reading the Bible could not be entirely prevented, Pope Benedict XIV., in 1757, nominally relaxed the prohibition; or as your divine, Dens (Theol. de Virtutibus, N. 64, t. ii. p. 103), expresses it, " Only where Catholics have to live among heretics has greater license been allowed."

The persecution of the Bishop of Pistoia, who desired to reform the Church, is well known. The Bull of 28th August 1794, of Pius VI., entitled, "Auctorem Fidei," against Bishop Ricci of Pistoia and his synod, condemns as " false and rash the doctrine that the union of the voice of the people with that of the Church was in accordance with God's counsels or apostolic practice," and that " nothing but weakness could excuse the reading of the Holy Scriptures." Is this enough ? If not, hear this. Clement VIII. and Gregory XIII. approved a translation by a Roman Catholic Jesuit priest, under an archbishop's direction ; an archbishop allowed this approved version of the Bible to be read by the people ; whereof another infallible Pope, Pius VII., successor to Clement and Gregory, thus writes, on 29th June 1816. Censuring the archbishop's conduct, he says, the version of the Bible in the vulgar tongue is " a most malignant invention, a pest, destructive of faith, the greatest danger for souls—a new kind of tares sown by the enemy, an impious conspiracy of innovators, the ruin of our holy religion." Were Clement VIII. and Gregory XIII. right when they approved and allowed, or was Pius VII. when he disapproved and disallowed, this one and the same version of the Bible ? and which Pope is infallible ? This was of an authorised version. No wonder, then, that the same Pope, Pius VII., in the same year, on 23d September 1816, should thus write to another archbishop, who had permitted in his diocese Bibles of the Bible Society: "We are greatly and deeply grieved at learning the fatal project, unknown in past time, of disseminating everywhere the Bible translated into the vulgar tongues; but our affliction was infinitely greater at seeing some letters, written in your name, exhorting the people to buy or accept these new versions of the Bible, and study them with attention and assiduity. Certainly nothing could occur more lamentable than to see you become a stone of offence—you, who ought to ask grace to show to others the way of righteousness."

Pope Leo XII., in the first year of his pontificate (3d May 1824), addressed to all archbishops and bishops of the Catholic Church his Encyclical Letter, saying, "To avert the plague of this most wicked novelty to both faith and morals," his predecessor, of "blessed memory, had sent the two briefs above mentioned to the archbishops;" and continues, "In conformity with our apostolic duty, we exhort you to turn away your flock by all means from these poisonous pastures. Reprove, beseech, be instant in season and out of season, that the faithful intrusted to you be persuaded that if the Sacred Scriptures be everywhere indiscriminately published, more evil than advantage will arise thence, on account of the rashness of men."

Twenty-seven Irish archbishops and bishops commended these infallible instructions of the Holy Father, "which prohibit the perusal of the Holy Scriptures in the vulgar tongue without the sanction of the competent authorities" (your "*proper dispositions*"), to the attention "of the faithful," as "replete with truth and wisdom;" adding, "such books have been and ever will be EXECRATED by the Catholic Church;" hence "she has frequently ordered them to be committed to the flames." These instructions were directed to be "read at times of Mass to the faithful by the clergy on successive Sundays."

Among those who signed the above were Archbishops Murray and Doyle. They stated, before a Committee of the House of Lords, that they had been educated, one in Spain and the other in Portugal, and that neither of them had ever seen a Spanish or Portuguese Bible; one had heard of the existence of one, and that was all he knew. Dr Doyle, in his examination, replied that, "he would refuse the Sacrament to a man who persisted in reading a Bible after prohibition;" that "he would be highly amused at a man who buried the Word of God;" and "he would reward the man for his proof of being filled with the right faith."

St Jerome, A.D. 384, wrote his "Vulgate" for the vulgar in the then vulgar tongue. In 1564, when Latin was no longer a living language, your Church pronounced that it alone should be read.

If the Bible was forbidden to be read in known languages, why was Jerome's, or the "innumerable translations" he mentions, made into known languages? Why did the Holy Ghost at Pentecost bestow the gift of tongues on the Church to impart Holy Writ, if Holy Writ in those tongues were by the Church to be denied, rejected, and proscribed?

Here I have brought down an unbroken chain of "infallible" and unimpeachable Roman Catholic evidence against reading the Bible, from the Council of Toulouse, in 1229, directed against the Waldenses and Albigenses, when Rome first began her war with the Bible, through the Council of Trent and massacre of the Huguenots to the present day, when the thunders of the Church are generally not always confined to anathemas.

You gave me your evidence to the contrary by stating that you had permission to have a Bible in your own cloisters, and you challenged me to the proof. I accepted the challenge on your own terms, i.e., to use the weapons which you should furnish. Surely in thus locking up the pure Word of God, and withholding Divine truth from her members, Rome has proved herself not infallible, but in error!

Persons may be disposed to ask, "What can be the reason why the Court of Rome thus objects to the perusal of the Bible? The latest authority I know in this country giving Rome's reasons, occurs (vide

Tablet, 4th April) in 1864, in the statement of Roman Catholic Bishop Goss of Liverpool, that "*the Bible is one of the most dangerous books that can be placed in the hands of the young.*"

My difficulty in adopting this is, that, if that be so, whether the devil was right or not, Jesus was clearly wrong when He answered and said, "Man shall live by every word that proceedeth out of the mouth of God" (Matt. iv. 4).

But the following reasons of "Christ's" ambitious "Vicar," to whom (*vide* Bull, "Unam Sanctam") "every human creature must be subject in order to be saved," are still more authoritative, and "savour" (Matt. v. 13) of the "tempter" (iv. 9), who said, "All these kingdoms of the world and the glory of them will I give thee"—on one condition.

The remarkable document which contains these reasons is to be found in the Imperial Library at Paris (folio B, No. 1038, vol. ii. pp. 641–650), also Brit. Mus. 7 c. 10, 11 "Fasciculus rerum," &c., (London, 1690, fol.), and is entitled "Advice of certain Bishops, assembled at Bologna, as to the mode of strengthening the Romish Church." It is difficult to understand how the cautious Court of Rome should suffer such a paper to see the light; though in the sixteenth century the connexion between the Court of France, under Catherine of Medici, with that of Rome, was very close. Catherine de Medici, you remember, instigated the massacre of 70,000 Protestants, which occurred within twenty years, viz., 1572. Besides, in the interval, the sacking and burning alive the inhabitants of Merindol and numerous atrocities, in celebration of which I possess a Papal medal with the inscription, "Solum in Belluas pius Bellator ferit."

The paper is a carefully-drawn answer to Pope Julius III., by three learned prelates whose counsel had been asked. It is dated " Bologna, 23d Oct. 1553," and signed " Vincentius de Durantibus, Episc. Thermulorum Brixiensis ; Egidius Falceta, Episc. Caprulen. ; Gherardus Busdragus, Episc. Thessal." They conclude their statement thus—" Lastly, of all the advice we can give your Beatitude, we have reserved to the end the most important, viz., that as little as possible of the Gospel (especially in the vulgar tongue) be read in all countries subject to your jurisdiction. That little which is usually read at Mass is sufficient, and beyond that no one whatever must be permitted to read. While men were contented with that little, your interests prospered, but when they read more, they began to decay. To sum all : that Book is the one which, more than any other, has raised against us those whirlwinds and tempests whereby we were almost swept away ; and, in fact, if any one examines it diligently, and then confronts therewith the practices of our Church, he will perceive the great discordance, and that our doctrine is utterly different from, and often even contrary to it ; which thing, if the people understand, they will not cease their clamour against us till all is divulged, and then we shall become an object of universal scorn and hatred. Wherefore, even those few pages must be put away, but with considerable wariness and caution, lest so doing should raise greater uproars and tumults."

Your reading " permitted in the vulgar tongue," while you were a member of a pure Christian Church, will enable you to " confront " this " advice " of your hierarchy to your chief Pontiff, how, with " craft " and " subtilty, for fear of the people," to quench the

"Light of the World," with that memorable occasion when, with scarcely greater impiety, "assembled together the Chief Priests and the Scribes to the Palace of the High Priest," and "consulted that they might take Jesus by subtilty and kill Him," "not on the feast-day, lest there be an uproar of the people."

I think you will be satisfied with these weapons from your own armoury, and will not desire me to go either further or elsewhere for more. I have shown you, on what you will accept as sufficient authority, how your holy Church, acting always, as she must, under the guidance, as you say, of the Holy Spirit, treats God's Word.

Can the doctrine propounded by your Roman theologians and cardinals be correct, viz., that "God and the Pope make one consistory"? or that "the Pope is more than God," or "another God upon earth"? (*Vide* note, p. 75.) Can this be correct? Be this as it may, in spite of God's commandments, against the authority of theologians, doctors, and fathers of the Christian Church, the infallible Pope forbids the reading of God's Word.

The faithful of Berea (Acts xvii. 11) were praised by the "Holy Spirit for comparing the word of the apostle with the word of God;" God's representative, who claims His Holy Spirit, condemns those who dare to confront the word of his Holiness, the apostles' pretended successor, with God's own Holy Word. St Peter and St John (Acts iv.), and the other apostles (Acts v.), told the high priest at Jerusalem, "We ought to obey God rather than men;" the high priest at Rome reverses the command, and says, "We ought to obey man more than God." Rome claims the support of St Augustine against reading the Bible ; St Augustine exhorts in various places to read it, and in his fifty-sixth Sermon states, " Be assured that as the body becomes when without food for some days, such becomes the soul when it does not feed often enough on the Word of God. Continue thus as usual to listen in the church, but read it also in your own houses."

Rome and you claim St Augustine's support when you observe that " the heretics say, 'Search the Scriptures.'" Have you forgotten ? You can scarcely ignore, still less denounce as " heretic," Christ, who enjoined (John v. 39) to " Search the Scriptures," which you forbid.

In an edition of the works of St Augustine published at Venice in 1584, public confession is made in the preface "that all those passages are removed which might favour the doctrines of the Protestants "—" in qua curavimus removeri ea omnia quae fidelium mentes hacretica pravitate possent inficere." The confession, at least, is candid.

The fact is, that the authority of all the fathers for twelve centuries (beginning with Clement of Rome, Polycarp, Irenæus, down to St Bernard in the twelfth) is in favour of the Bible.

You justify your keeping the Bible in an unknown tongue by reference to the Jews, who in their synagogues read the Old Testament in Hebrew. Hebrew is their language ; Latin is not yours. Their Bible was written in Hebrew ; yours was not written in Latin. Theirs is original ; yours a translation. They read the Bible in their houses, in the language where they are dispersed, and they learn Hebrew, and hope to be restored to Jerusalem. But if you accept the authority of the Jews as to the language of the books of Scripture, why do you reject their authority as to the books themselves? They are the keepers of the Old Testament: "To them (Rom. iii. 2) were intrusted the oracles of God." They retain, you reject, the Ten Commandments as God delivered them. They reject, you retain, the books of the Apocrypha. Your reason is manifest. You think therein to find, and forcibly though falsely extract, Divine authority for some of the worst but most lucrative abuses of your Church—Indulgences, Purgatory, &c.

Under Rome's claim to Infallibility, she both lengthens the Creed and shortens the Commandments. You object to that statement. I will prove it.

Do you know the Creed of Pope Pius IV. in 1564? That added to the Apostolic Creed the following articles, all unknown for six, most for twelve centuries of the Christian Church :—

	CIRCA A.D.
Traditions authorised in	1545
Constitutions and observances in the Church	1564
Five additional Sacraments (Council of Florence)	1439
Doctrines of Sin and Justification . .	1564
Transubstantiation (Council of Lateran) .	1225
Communion (forbidding the cup to laity) (Council of Constance) . . .	1414
Purgatory (Council of Florence) . .	1439
Indulgences, begun in 1200, confirmed .	1500
Supremacy of Rome	600
Obedience to Pope	600
Invocation of Virgin and Saints . .	1545
Veneration of Images	786
Veneration of Relics	786

Whatsoever Councils have declared or
    condemned   1564
Lastly, the Immaculate Conception of the
    Virgin, added by present Pope, Pius
    IX.   .   .   .   .   .

Surely this authoritative catalogue is a satisfactory proof of your lengthening the Creed.

In order to satisfy me that Rome does not shorten the Commandments, you send me a Catechism containing them as we have them, only differently divided, published under the authority of Cardinal Wiseman. Now this only proves the justice of the remark that Rome has double weights and double measures, one for show to Protestants, another for use to Catholics.

I possess another, headed " The Short Catechism, or what every Christian must know, containing exactly what the Church commands every one to know—Confession, Laws of God and of the Church, Rule of Life, Good Works, Sins, Conscience," and "published at one penny, under the authority of Cardinal Cullen, by Richardson and Sons, 147 Strand." It contains the Ten Commandments, not as in the Bible, but precisely as they are given in " The Most Complete Declaration of Christian Doctrine," composed by order of Pope Clement VII., an infallible authority, by Cardinal Bellarmine, revised and approved at Rome in 1841; and as this is a text-book for the instruction of those, like yourself, preparing for the priesthood, you will accept it as authentic.

It professes to give the Two Tables as they were delivered to Moses on Mount Sinai. .

The Divine truth is conveyed as follows :—

"*Disciple.* Let us now come to these very Commandments, and first teach me the identical words (*istesse parole*) in which they were written on those Tables by God.

"*Master.* The words are these :—

1. I am the Lord thy God, who brought thee out of the land of Egypt, and from the house of bondage. Thou shalt have no other God but me.
2. Thou shalt not take the name of the Lord thy God in vain.
3. Remember thou keep holy the festivals.
4. Honour thy father and thy mother.
5. Kill not.
6. Thou shalt not commit adultery.
7. Steal not.
8. Thou shalt not bear false witness against thy neighbour.
9. Thou shalt not covet thy neighbour's wife.
10. Thou shalt not covet thy neighbour's goods."

This, you observe, is no summary. They are promulgated as the "very words" your Church declares to be those contained in the 20th chapter of Exodus. Talk of mutilation by Protestants !

1. I would refer you to pp. 8–24 for a full explanation, which follows the Commandments in the Catechism, and to the "Moral Doctrines," which it states are from St Alphonso Liguori ; and as no saint can err in his writings, else Rome would not canonise him, these doctrines are infallibly correct.

In the two pages of explanation there is no allusion to devotion to idols, or to images ; but the "Christian" is told by St Alphonso Liguori "he must not go to prayers or sermons in Protestant places of worship ; and it would be a great sin to go when it is strictly forbidden ; " and as " a rule of life every day, if he can, he should visit (p. 38) some picture or image of the Blessed Virgin."

2. In explaining the Second Commandment, under the head of Oaths : " If you call God to witness that what you say is the truth, for example, 'I swear on the Book, or by the name of God, or the Holy Name—By heaven—On my soul—So help me God,' —if you do not mean to take an oath, then these words are no oath."

" It is not an oath to say, ' On my life—On my conscience—True as I stand here—True as Gospel —God's truth—God knows—I declare to God,' unless you mean these words for an oath."

This is the teaching of a Catechism for the young, for the uninstructed, the unconverted, prepared by a Catholic Priest (Rev. J. Furniss, Priest of Congregation of the M. H. Redeemer) under Cardinal Cullen, professing moral doctrines of a saint in the Romish Calendar, conveying God's " own words " to the laity from whom the Bible is withdrawn, and explaining the laws of God " exactly."

I cannot extract the whole, but under the head of " Murder " it teaches that " It is not a sin to desire some temporal misfortune to another, because it will make him cease to give scandal, or be converted or not persecute the good."

Under the " Seventh" (our Eighth) Commandment, p. 20, we find—" 1. It is a sin to steal, except in some cases of most grievous distress. . . . 2. It is a venial sin to steal a little. 3. It is a mortal sin to steal much. For example, to steal from a workman a day's wages, or to steal less from a poorer man, or more from a richer man. (If you steal from different persons, it needs half as much again for a mortal sin, and the same if you steal at different times. If you steal from different persons *as well* as at different times, it needs double the sum.)"

And under " Bargains or Contracts,"—" It is a sin to keep pieces which remain, except people are quite sure it is not against the will of the employer, or there is a common custom of doing it, and it is necessary in order to gain a reasonable profit. It is a sin to mix anything with what you sell, for example, water with any liquor, except there is a common custom of doing it, and it is necessary in order to gain a reasonable profit."

The Bible you forbid, commands to keep your word even to your own hurt or hindrance (Ps.' xv.) The morality of your Catechism teaches that "a promise does not oblige at all when things change so much afterwards that if you had foreseen it you would not have made the promise."

Few can credit how you are bound in chains, how you dread and hate the light ! " To go to hear a sermon in a Protestant Church is in itself Excommunication." " Ingressus in Protestantium templum animo concionis audiendi," is " Excommunicatio ipso facto " (*vide* printed Lists of Crimes in confessionals in Italian Churches), a crime reserved for the Bishop which the Priest cannot absolve.

Dr Newman, once a Protestant, now Professor of the Popish College in Ireland, gazetted by Fame as the next Cardinal, Prince of the Church (*vide* "Newman's Discourses," Longman, 1850, pp. 230–377), says, " The Church is the oracle of religious truth, and dispenses what the Apostles committed to her," and that " to open the Bible" (in the spirit of the Bereans

D

commended (Acts xvii.) by the Apostle) "is to disbelieve *her;*" "who doubts *her* teaching has fallen from grace and lost his faith ;" "hence she cannot allow her children the liberty of doubting the truth of her word ;" and adds, "Cease then to examine, or cease to call yourself her child."

Do you call this teaching scriptural? Your Church, to keep your calendar of saints select, employs at canonisation the officer quaintly termed the "Devil's Advocate," "Avocato del Diavolo." His client is "the Father of lies, and a Murderer from the beginning." The Advocate surely must have thought his client's interests would be advanced by admitting into heaven a candidate whose writings had the tendency of those of Alphonso de Liguori, d. 1787.

Your infallible Church sainted him in 1839. A saint cannot err in his works. Liguori suborns perjury, justifies false oaths, palliates fraud and treachery, excuses theft and robbery, allows injury to your neighbour, and even justifies self-murder, all "for ecclesiastical utility," and implies the greater the crime the higher the merit.

In your youth you learnt, and I know you still retain the following :—

Thou shalt do no murder.

Thou shalt not steal.

Thou shalt not bear false witness against thy neighbour.

Thou shalt not covet anything that is his (Exod. xx.), and "Thou shalt love thy neighbour as thyself."

These you know are "THE LAWS OF GOD."

"THE LAWS OF THE CHURCH," contained in the Catechism, are opposed to the Laws of God, but they are binding on you, and to doubt is infidelity.

St Alphonso's works are designed especially for the ignorant; they are published and widely circulated by authority of your Church as most excellent for the young, and are strongly recommended by Cardinal Wiseman.

The memory of good Christians deserves honour, and their lives to be recorded for example; but to my mind, this canonisation is simply blasphemously prejudging God's day of judgment.

Your "infallible" Pope enrols in Heaven a St Lucia or St Liguori, as demi-goddess or demi-god, by whose merit and influence you hope to be saved.

To mistrust your Church's decision, is the sin of infidelity, beyond other crimes and sins—and hereby God's throne is usurped, nor can God's decree reverse yours—else what becomes of your "infallibility?" Where is your ground of faith, of hope, of confidence, but in your Church? You annul the appeal to God, and it is no longer true that "we must *all* appear before the judgment-seat of Christ" (2 Cor. v. 10).

This, then, is the way in which the infallible Church of Rome abuses the Word of God, and falsely accusing others of the crime, herself first mutilates the laws, and then perverts their meaning.

I have always pitied the Roman Catholic laity who are prohibited by the priesthood to inquire or to exercise private judgment, and who have no means of comparing or controlling the teaching of their Church; but in proportion to my compassion for them is my contempt for those false teachers who have taken away the key of knowledge : and amid many trials not the least grief is that you should be found mixed up with those who palliate and propagate such dangerous and delusive doctrines.

It did require courage on your part to go to Rome, but that was a leap in the dark ; it may require courage to leave her and come out from her, but far more courage will it need to remain attached to such teaching. Were I in a court of justice thus to administer human laws, and from the bench to utter such monstrous doctrines of morality as those I have extracted from your authorised teaching, I know you would scorn and spurn me as an unjust judge. What then must be the inward feelings of your own conscience, not at reading but at venturing to approve, disseminate, and act upon such unholy doctrines of the holy Church ?

The teaching of Rome, as you declare it, is that she exults in possessing exclusively the right and the power of infallible decision.

Rome, which has mutilated the Scriptures, which has torn the Second Commandment from the Decalogue, which has placed creatures on the throne of heaven beside the Creator, which has falsified the Law given to Moses on Mount Horeb, ventures to copy and to travesty that glorious passage where on the same Mount Horeb " there was a wind that rent the mountains and brake in pieces the rocks, and after the wind an earthquake and a fire, and after the fire a still small voice, and when Elijah heard it he wrapped his face in his mantle."

Thus Rome declares, as you say—" The earth may quake, but let the still small voice of God be heard speaking through His chief representative, and each Catholic is hushed, he leaves his former thoughts, he rises up and " (as Elijah went and stood before the cave) " comes forth to listen in meekness and humility, he hears and he obeys in reverence and in silence."

The flesh creeps, shuddering and shivering, at this mockery. The matchless audacity, the unblushing hypocrisy, the blasphemy of this perversion of Holy Writ fill one with astonishment.

Is it to "God's Vicegerent on earth" you address the daily petition, "Thy will be done on earth"? You think, and will say, "No"—you practise "Yes."

On Mount Horeb the Law was given in the hearing of the whole nation of Israel, and afterwards written upon the tables of stone by the finger of God. To Mount Horeb Rome and you refer when you break that law ; to the voice of God you allude when you disobey His voice. And with this solemn and most holy authority you do not shrink to compare the fallible and unscriptural utterances of him you falsely call "God's chief representative."

In testimony you invoke the power of numbers ; you say Catholics double the Protestants.

Elijah said, "The prophets of Baal are four hundred and fifty men, and I, even I only, remain a prophet of the Lord."

According to Rome and you, Baal's prophets were right and Elijah false.

Elijah said, "I have been very jealous for the Lord God of Hosts."

Can you, dare you, when breaking the tables of stone, obliterating that very Law where the Lord says He is "a jealous God," appeal to Mount Horeb and say you fear God, you love God, or that you observe His statutes to keep them ?

"I know you are incapable."

I have shown many inconsistencies in your Church, but any one inconsistency, any single error, established and brought home to the Pope and Church of Rome, is fatal to her claim to Infallibility, and if that fall, the whole system follows.

NEXT, I charge the Church of Rome and her followers with the sin of Idolatry. Let us not mince the matter. Here she is like the woman taken in adultery, in the very act. It is in vain for casuists to draw the refined distinction between *latreia* and *duleia*. You have only to visit a Roman Catholic Church to satisfy yourself that the sin of idolatry is committed every day by nine out of ten of the worshippers. They bow down and fix their eyes upon the work of men's hands, images and pictures in which they believe a divine and miraculous power to exist; in other words, where the Divinity actually is. Hence all the worship is formal, ceremonial, sensual. And is not this just what the Hindoo, the Buddhist, and the idolater of Africa go through in their forms of worship? They require some material object in order that they may offer prayer to it.

Hard words do no good, but there are some points on which the truth, however painful, ought to be told. Pagans have the excuse of heathen darkness. Rome has the greater crime of putting out the light in order to commit the sin. I charge Rome plainly with idolatry—gross, wilful idolatry—alike in doctrine and in practice.

I cannot describe to you how inexpressibly distressing it is to me thus to address you, exceeded only by the pain of seeing you thus drawn into the vortex into which it will be your duty to decoy and lead others from the religion of Jesus to nothing short of idolatry, under the guise of the religion of Mary and the worship of the saints. And this in disobedience to God, in obedience to His "chief representative," your "Vicegerent of God upon earth," your "Alter Deus" (other God), as one theologian, your "plusquam Deus" (more than God), as another blasphemously styled him ; your Pope, " Moses in authority, Peter in dignity, Christ himself in office " (Pius VI., Brev. Rom. Paris, 1775), who when elected is seated not on St Peter's pretended chair, but literally enthroned (like God) upon God's high altar in the chief cathedral of St Peter, and who thence is borne aloft in triumph, after adoration ("Adorant quem creant," Papal medal) of the cardinals, princes of the Church, around the sacred building, shrouded with feathered screens like seraphs' wings, emblematic of that high and holy Being who inhabiteth eternity, in whose sight the very heavens are not clean, and whom angels worship with folded wings.

I know you are incapable of designedly deceiving on any point, much less on a subject so solemn as an article of belief ; and therefore, like very many others, you are yourself, though honest, deceived in regard to the Virgin-worship not being *latreia* or adoration, equal and like that offered to God Himself. I know you term it the mediation of intercession ; and to such an extent do your bishops carry this doctrine, that they teach that the tempest on the Sea of Tiberias was calmed by our Saviour, not at the request of the disciples, but at the instigation of His mother. Dr Grant, R. C. Bishop of Southwark, in his recent Pastoral Letter, said : " Mary could again urge her Divine Son to rise up and bid the winds and the waves be calm."

I see on highest authority, and by daily custom, that the real practice of worship to the saints, and especially the Virgin, is to give them, and her in particular, more praise and greater worship than is given to God. Throughout Italy, whether in churches, chapels, shrines, or wayside crosses, it is ever the Virgin who is most prominent; it is to her almost exclusively, and not to God, that prayers are directed to be addressed. The business of the people is, as they are shown and taught, not with God, but with the Virgin and with the saints. The other day at Pisa I read on the door of a principal church a proclamation in which God was neither named nor alluded to, calling on the people "to pay especial worship to the Virgin, because she [not Almighty God], as Queen of Heaven, had last year saved the city from the cholera, when so many fell victims to it in the neighbouring town of Leghorn." And this is the prevailing custom. When the cholera arrived in Europe above thirty years since, a prayer was written for the use of the members of the Gallican Church at Lyons, containing no mention of the providence of Almighty God, but supplications only to the Blessed Virgin to save the town by her " sweet breath."

You direct me to the Litany to the Virgin and the Office to the Virgin, to show that it is honour, not worship — intercession, not mediation — respect, not prayer—which is offered to the Virgin, and that I only exhibit my own ignorance, not the tenets of you and your Church, by calling the Virgin " mediatrix." If it be ignorance, it is that I did not assert more and place the Virgin still higher, actually as Queen of Heaven, for to her is offered the highest kind of worship, to her are dedicated the most direct prayer and supplication, and her position eclipses the Creator and Redeemer.

I find these words in the " Officium parvum B. Mariæ," " Deliver us always from all dangers, glorious and blessed Virgin." I commend you also to the following Litany in the Catechism published by authority of Cardinal Cullen :—

> "Heart of Jesus, I adore thee ;
> Heart of Mary, I implore thee ;
> Heart of Joseph, pure and just ;
> In *these three* Hearts I *put my trust.* Amen."

A Pope is infallible. Pius IX., writing from Gaeta, February 2, 1849, in his Encyclic Letter, says—"You know full well, venerable brethren, that all ground of our confidence is placed in the Most Holy Virgin, since God has placed the fulness of all good in her ; so that if there be in us any hope, any grace, any salvation, we may know that it flows from her, because such is the will of *Him* who wills that we should have all through Mary."

Who is He? (Luke xi. 27, 28.) "A certain woman of the company lifted up her voice and said unto HIM, Blessed is the womb that bare thee, and the paps which thou hast sucked. But HE said, Yea, rather blessed are they that hear the word of God and keep it."

You ask my authority for terming Mary a mediatrix. Pius IX., in his allocution to the Secret Consistory, 25 September 1865, writes—"In order that our vows may be heard, let us pray to our mediatrix with the all-clement God, the Most Holy Virgin, that Mother immaculate from her birth, to whom it has been granted to overthrow the enemies of our Church and monstrous errors."

Read the following under the picture of the Virgin at the corner of the Convent of St Sylvester, in Via d. Mercede, Rome—"Lady, save thy people." Or the conclusion of the prayer suspended on the rails of the Chapel of St Mary, " Consoler of the afflicted,"— " Deliver me from all evil," &c. Or the following prayer, published at Rome, 1825, with "the license of superiors," "dispensed gratis by order of Pope Pius VII.," dated 19th July 1822, "with indulgence to those reciting it," the order signed by Cardinal Galeffi :—

> "I adore you, eternal Father, &c.
> I adore you, eternal Son, &c.
> I adore you, Most Holy Spirit, &c.
> I adore you, Most Holy Virgin, &c."

This is not merely invocation, veneration, or inter-cession, but adoration ; there is none of the distinction you imagine, but actual worship, at least equal to that of the Trinity. You can hardly believe that it is other-wise, and therefore will not convince me nor try to persuade others against the fact that the Virgin not only is worshipped, but worshipped more than God. Nor is it perceptible or intelligible that this worship is only intercessorial. The people do not and cannot un-derstand it so. The Queen of Heaven is supreme with you.

You refer me to the Litany to the Virgin to show me that you only ask the Virgin to pray for us—" Ora pro nobis." That is not all. In Prayers to which in-dulgences are attached (Rome, with authority, 1844), in Missal for Use of Laity, in Roman Breviary, in Service of the Mass, and, as you know well, in numer-ous Offices, forgiveness of sins is asked " through the merits of " the Virgin.

You know by the Sabbatine Bull of Pope John XXII., published in March 1822, confirmed by other apostolic Bulls, the Virgin goes regularly every

"Saturday," and "as soon as possible" on other days, to "bring out of the flames of purgatory to eternal joy in paradise those who wear" (on their shoulder her livery) "her holy scapular." (*Vide* Indulgences, &c., conferred on the Order, &c., of the Virgin Mary of Mount Carmel. Dublin, 1826. Bull re-published by Gregory XVI. in 1841.) And this the Virgin can do of her own non-mediatorial power ! ! !

The works of saints are free from error, and "are written for YOUR learning," and enjoined while the Bible is forbidden. Read this and shudder. SAINT Bernardine and SAINT Alphonso de Liguori, canonised 1839, declare, and you are bound to accept and teach it as free from error, that the Virgin "enjoys the same privileges" as God ; "that power may be EQUAL between the Son and the Mother;" "that Jesus rendered Mary *omnipotent;*" that "as many creatures serve the glorious Virgin Mary as serve the Trinity." That is not all, "even God Himself is SUBJECT to the command of the Virgin."

To us this seems incredible! but if this be right, no wonder SAINT Anselm should assure us "our prayers will often be more speedily heard by invoking Mary than calling on Jesus." No wonder that another saint, whose works are a favourite class-book, SAINT Bonaventura (Psalter to Blessed Virgin), should invert the Psalms of David and address them to the Virgin. The CXth Psalm, named by St Matthew, St Mark, St Luke, and St Paul, and quoted by our Lord as prophesying the Messiah, is applied to Mary—"The Lord said unto my Lady, Sit thou on my right hand," &c., and so throughout. Thus too the SAINT travesties that glorious Canticle, the Te Deum—"We praise thee, O Mary," &c. And in some editions even the

Lord's Prayer itself becomes " Our Lady which art in heaven, Hallowed be thy name,", &c. Admitting she is a creature, you assign to Mary the three attributes of Godhead, Omnipotence, Omniscience, and Omnipresence.

Are not you a Romanist, terrified when you read that passage in St Matt. iv. 10, and that of St Paul to the Romans (Rom. i. 25), denouncing those "who changed the truth of God into a lie, and worshipped and served the creature more than the Creator"?

Reflect a moment too upon the effect which all this honour and adulation offered to her must have upon the Virgin herself. Worthy of the highest reverence, deserving of the most tender affection as the mother of our Blessed Saviour, we can meditate upon no mortal with respect equal to that we owe to the Virgin. Her humble, modest, lovely character, her highly-favoured person, her meek and gentle spirit, claim from us more than is due to any other human being. Inasmuch as nothing is more characteristic of meanness and dishonesty than to assume dignity which does not belong to you, or to take credit for favours you have not granted, so nothing is more revolting to a noble mind, or abhorrent to truth or generous character, than to receive honours to which it has no right, titles to which it has no claim, and gratitude for acts not done. Consider, then, the position in which your adulation places the lowly Mary, whose own words, "rejoicing in God her Saviour," deny and disprove what you pretend (Luke i.)

Can you now say the Virgin in your Church is not worshipped as a God? Let that for argument be granted. Then it is worse. Her worship then is not as a God, but as a creature.

Your Church does not stop here. Not only the Virgin is worshipped, but her pictures are endowed with the power of vision, and of uttering her thoughts and wishes. "On the 9th of July 1846 (*vide* Diario Romano) was invoked the patronage of the Most Holy Virgin in memory of the wonderful movement of the eyes observed in many of her images in the year 1796." This is announced under the authority of your Church.

The Bible records two remarks of the Blessed Virgin, one after the Child Jesus disputed with the doctors, the other at the marriage at Cana, when our Lord replied, "Woman, what have I to do with thee?" From the commencement of His ministry, no other saying is recorded either by holy apostles or holy fathers, until we come to the conversation which is inscribed in Latin and in Italian in the church of St Damian at Rome.

The conversation occurred in the church, between the Virgin and St Gregory, Pope (circa A.D. 720), and is recorded as follows : "The image which is on the high altar said to St Gregory, Pope, 'Why do you no longer salute me, as in passing you were wont to salute me?' The Saint begged pardon, and conceded to those, who celebrate on that altar, the liberation of the soul from purgatory, that is of that soul for which the Mass is celebrated." The Virgin also spoke to Pope John XXII., about 1320, and told him she visited Purgatory every Saturday, as narrated infallibly in the Bull confirmed in 1822.

And in last century the Virgin held frequent conversations with Alphonso Liguori, but the Saint unfortunately does not tell us what she said, only that they were "such sweet things!"

The heathen mythology, their worship of gods and goddesses, and their introduction and adoration of statues of Venus, of Juno, and Diana, was copied by and remains in Rome. The pagan converts, and such as would have sacrificed to Paul and Barnabas, associated with the image an idea of a divinity, and though (Minutius Felix, 123) it was reproached to the primitive Christians, as Romanists reproach Protestants, that they had no images, and the Councils of Laodicea (A.D. 352), and Elvira, and Constantinople condemned the practice, yet Rome adopted and enjoined the idolatry.

What can be more impious than the following, sanctioned under the eye of the Vicar of God, and which you probably have seen? A doll, representing the infant Saviour, which any day can be seen in its box by strangers for a few francs, and which is termed the "Bambino of the Ara Cæli Church," takes its airing in a procession with two (formerly with four) horses, and accompanied by footmen. This "image, enriched with emeralds, sapphires, topazes," I quote a Catholic authority, "amethysts, diamonds, and other precious ornaments," is taken from its box when sent for in certain cases of illness, and placed on the patient's bed, who on recovery is expected to, and does, pay well for the performance.

Is not this wicked imposture and gross idolatry matchless in Christendom?

Mr Faber, in his recent work on the Lives of Modern Saints, strongly commended by Cardinal Wiseman, narrates among innumerable marvels, that when other medicines had failed, an infusion of powdered or grated saints' bones taken inwardly, effected a surprising cure.

I shall not dwell on relic veneration, of which the list is endless, and the lucrative imposture, if not impious, would be ludicrous. I give a few relating to the Blessed Virgin in some churches at Rome :—

Church of Holy Cross . . " One bottle of the milk of the Most Blessed Virgin."

St Mary Transpontina . " Some of the milk of the Blessed Virgin Mary."

St Cosmo and Damian . . " One bottle of the milk of the Blessed Virgin Mary."

St Cecilia Trastevere . . " Some milk of ditto, and great toe of St Mary Magdalen."

St John Lateran ⎱ . . . " Some hair and clothing
inter alia ⎰   of the Blessed Virgin Mary ; the veil of the Virgin with which the same succeeded with difficulty in covering the nakedness of her only Son, whilst He hung on the wood of the Cross, still sprinkled with some drops of blood."

(Copied from Lists of Relics hung up in the churches.)

I pass over the bones of Abraham, Isaac, and Jacob, and the stone upon which Isaac was offeted, which, along with Aaron's beard, are at Rome, together with his rod, which is at Rome and also at Paris and Bologna ; the entire skeletons of several of the apostles existing both at Rome and at several other churches, and many of their bones in other places ; but the following is really so shocking that one blushes to narrate it. In this century was published, with approbation at Rome, in 1802, a "Critical Historical Narrative of the most precious relic of the most sacred Foreskin of our Lord Jesus Christ, venerated in the parish church of Calcata." The book relates that the Virgin, having preserved it, gave it on her ascension to Mary Magdalen or to St John, and they to others ; that some angels found it and gave it to Charlemagne ; that afterwards it came into the possession of a soldier in the army of the Emperor Charles V., and at length it discovered itself in a miraculous manner, and it is now exposed in church for the adoration of the faithful.

I confess Indulgences to be beyond my comprehension. How any sane man can suppose that with the Almighty he can have, as it were, a running account, and by paying a few shillings or saying a few more Aves or Pater Nosters than usual he can show a large balance in hand, and spare a portion to place to the credit of the souls of the dead if he pleases, surpasses my understanding.

Pope Borgia (Alexander VI.) first, *ex cathedrâ*, released souls from Purgatory by indulgences (Ranke, Book I., cap. ii.)

In the "appartamento Borgia" of the palace of God's Vicegerent, over a doorway, is a "*Holy Virgin and*

Infant Jesus in a glory of angels, with a saint adoring."
Vasari says the "Saint was Pope Borgia," the "lady"
the adored "Julia Farnese," his mistress. Did Cæsar
Borgia represent the Saviour in this picture of un-
exampled blasphemy and depravity ? Borgia might
well seek power to deliver souls, but can a pure
stream flow from so foul a source ? and you will
hardly welcome this origin of a doctrine now (Council
of Trent, Sess. 25, cap. 21) an article of your new
faith.

Indulgences were instituted to decoy, and deceive,
and extract money. They and relics were found to
be such a lucrative traffic for buying and selling souls,
that though, under the direction of the Holy Office,
commissioners have tried to regulate the market, the
infallible Church has found it advantageous to let the
sale go on. I think I am correct in this matter, and
that my understanding of it probably equals yours ;
but I should be glad to know whether the following
table, not of fees, but charges, payable for indulgences
or absolution of crime, at the office of the Supreme
Pontiff, still holds good as it did a short time since :—

	£	s.	d.
Pardon of a heretic . . .	36	9	0
„ for marrying one wife after murder of another . . .	8	2	9
„ for robbery . . .	0	12	0
„ „ simony . . .	0	10	6
„ „ seduction . . .	0	9	0
„ „ incest . . .	0	7	6
„ „ murder . . .	0	7	6

Have the rates been altered ?   I have extracted
the list from Dr Hook's "Church Dictionary," a work

E

of much research and erudition, but as he gives the reference you can satisfy yourself at Rome as to the correctness.

The money value, the amount, is of less moment, the material point is that you, a man, and your priest claim to have a power, for money, to do what God declares cannot be done for money, and to do that which belongs to God alone. Our Lord says how hard it is for a rich man to enter the kingdom of Heaven ; your Church reverses that doctrine.

There are many other articles of creed, doctrines and tenets of your Church, equally irreconcilable with scriptural authority or common sense. They have often been argued and controverted, and are only maintained in your Church by the complete systematic discipline which enforces obedience by blind submission to whatever the Church declares.

You cannot marvel or complain at the charge that your Church makes what is true appear false, or what is false appear true. The " Lord's Supper," represented by the Mass, was not taken fasting, and the cup denied by you was given to " all after supper."

By your principles and practice, as God's mercy is not boundless, so is not His power infinite. The merits of Christ, the mercy of God, are in the hands, the mind, not of God but of man, dispensed or reserved, given or withheld, not at God's will, but at your, or any sinful priest's option, who by fasting or not fasting after midnight, by intending [a] or not intending it, may make good or make void the Consecration of the Element, and make or mar the miracle of the Mass—all depends on the intention of the priest—his caprice, his failing, his fraud, nay, even

[a] Co. Trent on Intention (Sess. 7, cap. 11).

his malice may annul the efficacy of the Sacrament.

Your Pope, your Vicegerent of God upon earth, is too modest and unassuming in his titles! Not he alone, but every miserable priest is not only "alter Deus in terrâ," but "plusquam Deus." In daily significance and application, the primeval Creation dwindles to nothing beside your mediæval discovery, "Sacerdos creat Deum."

You desired me to obtain information of your practice from your own authorities. The task has been grievous and loathsome, and for your sake, I have with heavy heart endeavoured to fulfil what you bade. I could have extended it, for the work is endless ; but enough has been done to exhibit a picture of fearful blasphemy and gross idolatry, and to show that your Church, subversive of infallibility, is full of error, and destructive of Unity, applies to practice and to profession double weights and double measures.

This may avail for profit here, but I doubt if such conduct will serve before that Judge who is about your bed and about your path, and spieth out all your ways, who searcheth the hearts and who hateth a lie, in that Court of last resort from which there is no appeal, where human infallibility is unknown, where idolatry is condemned, where no more indulgences are granted, where no earthly penances are counted, and where the Pope requires, but can no longer offer, absolution.

I have shown that in profession with Protestants you pretend to permit the Bible, in practice with your people you proscribe and prohibit it. Quoting Deut. xvii. 12, "That false Prophets should be slain," St

Thomas Aquinas, your "Angelic Doctor," says,
"Forgers of faith," meaning Protestants, "may be
punished, as forgers of money may be put to death."
Mutilating Scripture and misquoting it, as it was
quoted to our Saviour on the Mount, you proclaim
that we pervert and that you alone preserve Holy
Writ. To clip and deface sterling coin is a great
crime, falsely to charge others with such conduct is a
greater ; to do so in order to withdraw genuine and
forge or utter spurious metal as true is most base, em-
phatically infamous in those at the mint who are
charged to ensure its being genuine. Of this we con-
vict the Church of Rome. She falsifies the truth and
accuses others of the crime in order with impunity to
commit it herself. With inconceivable blasphemy,
she cites as witness the Holy Ghost, and alleges His
inspiration in attestation of perjury and fraud.

The proofs are drawn from the writings, not of
Reformers, but of divines of your own Church, showing your doctrines from your own doctors, arguing
your Creed from your own authorities. If I have
worked with earnestness, I have also with calmness ;
if I have studied with anxiety, I have also with con-
sideration ; impressed, indeed, with deep solicitude
and hope for men who, like you, embraced the tenets
of Rome ere you could know her teaching or her practice, but with faint expectations of effect on many who,
reflecting little, are relieved from that little by a
Church excluding thought or reason or right of private judgment.

It is true that the Papacy has abated nothing since
Rome gave Ireland to Henry II. of England in A.D.
1272, or England to Philip of Spain in A.D. 1587 ; she
still absolves subjects from obedience. Her organ in

this country, the *Tablet*, lately stated that laws affecting Catholics which (in addition to the Royal) have not received the Papal assent are null and void, or, as it states, " have not the value of a tenpenny nail." It is true that Archbishop Manning, on opening St Mary's Chapel at Leeds, Sept. 13, 1866, declared "that God had given the Pope supremacy of direction and guidance over all other powers on earth." Statesmen may pay little regard to religion, but he must be a careless observer of passing events in England who does not perceive the recent political progress of Popery. Romanism admits of connexion with no state save that of Rome. That state establishment suppressed but never extinguished, claims never to have ceased. You Romanists see and smile, but forbear to say that Protestantism disestablished is Romanism re-established, as significantly and as surely as a lamp, unnoticed while daylight fills the chamber, becomes the light when sunshine is excluded. Thus " lanterns and torches " (John xviii. 3) may burn unseen, and men only follow their glare when the lamp of heaven, " the light of the world," is shut out. Unchanging Rome's claims and pretensions, like her doctrines, are kept ever alive and ready for use. Thus "the Pope— (so his legate told the council)—as vicar of Christ, who is lord of all things, is lord of all temporal domains, even as domains belong to men under God." Thus " princes should purge their dominions of all heretics, and extinguish them to the utmost of their power." The fourth Lateran council requires this. But the question with you regards less Rome's temporal than her spiritual aggression. My charge is that Rome prefers darkness to light, ignorance to knowledge, falsehood to truth, human doctrines to Divine laws, superstition to religion, slavery to freedom, immorality to purity, idolatry to holy worship, and that you are bound to have and teach it so.

I appreciate and reciprocate the affectionate earnestness with which you warn me, ere it be too late, to quit a Church in which there is no salvation. The picture you give is graphic. You write : " If you, sailing over the ocean in a big ship, see me in a rotten little boat, in the delusion that I shall come in safety to the journey's end, it is no charity to cheer me, but rather it is charity to say to me, ' You cannot be saved in your boat ; come up hither.' "

No doubt it would be kindly meant, but you might be mistaken both as to the rottenness of my frail bark and the seaworthiness of your showy three-decker.

I might reply : "Your ship is very high out of the water, is beautifully painted, and has plenty of hands, but your charts are not correct, your compass is out of order, your Captain is not infallible, and it is not always the biggest craft that is the safest ; and, I confess, frail and tempest-tossed as may be my little boat, I had rather continue my stormy and anxious passage in her, at times covered with waves, with the needle pointing heavenward, with the Cross for my flag, with Jesus for my pilot, and the fishermen of Galilee for my mariners, than enjoy the luxuries of your great, showy, and gaudy ship, assured that when the storm was at the highest there might yet be a great calm ; and, listening to the cheering voice, ' Why are ye fearful ? ' I should trust to reach the haven without shipwreck."

I always gladly seek the points, not of divergence

but of convergence, in the Churches of England and of Rome. We are too far apart, and if each of us were nearer Christ we should be nearer each other. There are in the Anglo-Catholic Church some whom I may term Roman Catholic call-ducks, who think that the chief difference is one of ceremonial. Some favourable to extreme Ritualism, not unfavourable to Romanism, whose faith is in themselves, who take mysticism for depth of thought, subtlety for reason, and outward form for religion ; and others, who are attracted by the gorgeous display, mistake that for devotion, and fancy if we adopted your vestments, your ornaments, and your processions, there would be small difference between the two Churches. I am not one of them! No one desires unity more than myself, but unity must be second to truth, not truth to unity, and unity must rest on the basis, not of fiction or fancy, but of God's Word.

You discourse upon these points with me, nay, you challenge me to discuss them on your own terms. I have little more to add ; but before I conclude I beg you to consider what in your conscience and belief is really " the one faith divinely revealed," and in what position by her doctrine Rome places God's Word and God's Spirit. God's Spirit is in the Bible—God's Spirit is in the Pope.

The one says, "Search the Scripture ; " the other, " Search them not."

The one, " Compare them with the Church's teaching ; " the other, " Confront them at your peril."

The one, " You shall add nothing thereto ; " the other, " You shall add."

The one, " You shall take nought from the Commandments ; " the other, " You shall."

Which do you believe ?

The one, " You shall only worship God ; " the other, " Worship creatures as well as the Creator."

I might multiply these traditions which lead only to infidelity.

Rome says, " God's Spirit is in the Pope or in his Councils" (Pope Pius IX., Syllabus, Dec. 8, 1864).

The Laodicean and Chalcedon Councils reject the Apocrypha ; at Trent the Council cursed him who rejects it. Yet it is God who lieth not (Titus).

At Constantinople (A.D. 754) the Council denies the corporeal presence ; at Lateran, at Constance, and at Basle declares it.

The Pope excommunicated St Augustine, and so he died ; the Pope made him a Saint.

The Pope excommunicated Cyprian, and so he died ; the Pope canonised St Cyprian.

Councils condemned image worship in A.D. 754, and approved it in 787.

Pope Liberius approved of the Arian heresy ; Pope Vigilius taught the heresy of Eutyches ; Councils of the Church condemned both.

Was the Holy Ghost in the Pope John XXIII., and also in the Council of Constance which deposed him from the Papacy ?

The Councils of Constance and Basle set Councils above the Pope ; the Council at Lateran set the Pope above Councils.

Was the Holy Ghost in one Pope at Rome and in another at Avignon, while each was denouncing the other as Antichrist ?

Was the Holy Ghost at one moment in three antagonistic Popes at once ?

The Bible says no apostle shall be before or after

other; the Pope says St Peter was prince of the apostles.

The Word of God, in the Eucharist, says, "Drink ye all of this;" the Pope says, "Save the priests, drink none of ye of this."

Scripture says, "Feed my sheep;" the shepherd says, "Your food is poison."

Scripture says, "I will lead you into green pastures;" the shepherd says, "Your pastures are deadly."

The good Shepherd (John xvii. 17) says, "Sanctify them through thy truth, thy word is truth;" the Pope, your shepherd, replies, "Your word does more harm than good."

Your boasted Unity—Unity not in the Church, much less oneness with Christ—tends to and ends in this hideous and impious deformity. Amid this puzzling perplexity and "infallible" confusion, where both are true, where "under pain of condemnation" "both must be believed" (Syllabus of Pope Pius IX.), which is to be followed—the order, or the counter-order? Which is to be trusted,—what your Church affirms, or what she denies? what she commands, or what she forbids?

Where now is that "ONE POSITIVE, DEFINITE BE-LIEF DIVINELY REVEALED," in search of which you left us and went to Rome, which you assert Rome teaches and we do not, which she "positively enforces as necessary to salvation, which it is a *sin against God* to doubt, and which was held by all," says Rome, "till the idea of private judgment," which you pretend began at the Reformation, but really approved at Berea, "was started"?

F

Is it only in your "infallible" Pius IX., your "Noster Deus Papa," "our God the Pope," as styled at the Council of Lateran, Sess. 4; in your "*Earthen Vessel containing the Divine Treasure*," as Rome and you declare? Truly "of the earth, earthy!"

You will hardly venture again, as if exclusively possessing our true pure faith, tauntingly and exultingly to ask me, "What is that body of faith of which a Church can, like Rome, rise up and say, without qualification of any kind, 'This I believe!' 'This is the faith which has always been held!' 'This is the faith of the apostles!'"

Your infallibility has incorporated blasphemy, lies, fraud, idolatry, and abominations, therefore all these are right. If wrong, where is your infallibility?

I am no theologian, much less a Jesuit in argument, but no argument, no artifice, no Jesuitical casuistry can reconcile these conflicting "infallible" truths if your Church be true, or can justify her if she be not.

Yet many like you in England are now busy in putting the Breviary in place of the Bible, are now engaged in uprooting "the tree of life" for that "in the midst of the garden," and say they are "doing God service."

I pray that the Spirit of God may guide you into all truth, and may lead you to retrace your steps and to flee from the judgment which will, as I understand the apocalyptic vision of St John, surely overtake those who not only defile and defy His laws but use them as a means of corrupting those they undertook to teach. Though now "joined to idols," you may, like Ephraim, "be left alone." Remember the fate of the disobedient Prophet, and the denunciations against those who took away the key of knowledge, who entered not in themselves nor suffered those to go in who would. You have driven me to track your Church's dark and devious course, and your feeble efforts to deaden your conscience as to Infallibility and its consequences.

I have written as I had not intended—painfully, laboriously, and at length—led on by the intense interest of a subject so important, and of the fearful consequences to those who err and who mislead.

That God may guide you and me aright is the very earnest prayer of

Your anxiously affectionate

FRANCIS SCOTT.

NOTE TO P. 35.

Bible printed with authority, 1723.

NOTE TO P. 36.

There are many other Papal Decrees against the Bible.

NOTE TO P. 43.

Such were the titles ascribed to Popes by Cardinals Cajetan and Bellarmine.

BALLANTYNE AND COMPANY, PRINTERS, EDINBURGH.